PRODUCED BY

PRESIDENT: Julie Merberg
EDITORIAL DIRECTOR: Sarah Parvis
EDITORIAL ASSISTANT: Sara DiSalvo
DESIGNED BY: Georgia Rucker Design
SPECIAL THANKS: Brian Michael Thomas, Krissy Roleke

PUBLISHER: Bob Der
EDITOR, TIME FOR KIDS MAGAZINE: Nellie Gonzalez Cutler
PROJECT EDITOR: Andrea Delbanco

PUBLISHER: Jim Childs
VICE PRESIDENT, BRAND & DIGITAL STRATEGY: Steven Sandonato
EXECUTIVE DIRECTOR, MARKETING SERVICES: Carol Pittard
EXECUTIVE DIRECTOR, RETAIL & SPECIAL SALES: Tom Mifsud
EXECUTIVE PUBLISHING DIRECTOR: Joy Butts
DIRECTOR, BOOKAZINE DEVELOPMENT & MARKETING: Laura Adam
FINANCE DIRECTOR: Glenn Buonocore
ASSOCIATE PUBLISHING DIRECTOR: Megan Pearlman
ASSOCIATE GENERAL COUNSEL: Helen Wan
ASSISTANT DIRECTOR, SPECIAL SALES: Ilene Schreider
SENIOR BOOK PRODUCTION MANAGER: Susan Chodakiewicz
DESIGN & PREPRESS MANAGER: Anne-Michelle Gallero
BRAND MANAGER: Jonathan White
ASSOCIATE PREPRESS MANAGER: Alex Voznesenskiy
ASSOCIATE PRODUCTION MANAGER: Kimberly Marshall
ASSISTANT BRAND MANAGER: Stephanie Braga
EDITORIAL DIRECTOR: Stephen Koepp
SPECIAL THANKS: Katherine Barnet, Jeremy Biloon, Rose Cirrincione, Jacqueline Fitzgerald, Christine Font, Jenna Goldberg, Hillary Hirsch, David Kahn, Amy Mangus, Nina Mistry, Dave Rozzelle, Ricardo Santiago, Adriana Tierno, Vanessa Wu

WELCOME TO TOP 5 OF EVERYTHING

The fastest! ... through these ... ever the largest, ... ost popular things in ... m, in space, in school, ... d the world. We've tried ... onstag... to make it clear whenever there is a TIE —these lists feature more than five people, places, or things. We've also worked hard to use the most up-to-date statistics available at the time of printing. Enjoy!

—The Editors of TIME FOR KIDS

Biggest • Longest • Oldest • Most-photographed • Hottest • Youngest • Smartest • Sugariest • Tallest • Best-selling • Most populous • Best • Strongest • Highest-paid • ... • ...ungest • Most-played • Deepest • Most common • Sleep... • ... • Friendliest • Longest-running • Fastest • Warmest • Most p... • ...est • Most popular • Greatest • Smartest • Biggest • Long... • ...st-photographed • Snowiest Heaviest • Smartest • Be... • ... Tallest • Most populous • Hottest • Strongest • Col... • ...Most-played • Best-selling Deepest • Sleepiest • Tastiest • ... • ...unning • Highest-paid • Snowiest • Fastest • War... • ...reatest • Most-produced • Longest • Smartes... • ...tographed • Sleepiest Most-played • You... • ...ariest • Tallest • Hottest • Stronge... • ... • Best-selling Best • Deepest • ... • ...hest-paid • Snowiest • Fastes... • ... • Friendliest Biggest • Longest • ... • ...Youngest • Smartest • Sugar... • ... • Best • Strongest • Highes... • ...Deepest • Most-produced • ... • ...unning • Fastest • Warmest • M... • ...Greatest • Smartest • Biggest • L... • ...Snowiest Youngest • Smartest • ... • ...opulous • Hottest • Strongest • C... • ...Best-selling Deepest • Sleepiest • Tasties... • ...Highest-paid • Snowiest • Fastest • Warmest... • ...Most common • Longest • Smartest • Biggest • Ol... • ...ographed • Sleepiest Most common • Youngest • Smartest • Coldest • Sugariest • Tallest • Hottest • Strongest • Snowiest • Heaviest • Most-played • Best-selling

Fastest U.S. Roller Coasters

If you like amusement parks, hold on to your hats! Roller coasters are bigger and faster than ever. Some can travel as fast as trains!

 Kingda Ka

Six Flags Great Adventure
Jackson, New Jersey
128 miles (206 km) per hour

Source: Roller Coaster Database

2. Top Thrill Dragster
Cedar Point
Sandusky, Ohio
120 miles (193 km) per hour

3. Escape from Krypton
Six Flags Magic Mountain
Valencia, California
100 miles (161 km) per hour

4. Millennium Force
Cedar Point
Sandusky, Ohio
93 miles (150 km) per hour

5. Intimidator 305
Kings Dominion
Doswell, Virginia
90 miles (145 km) per hour

TOP 5 OLDEST BASEBALL STADIUMS

1. **Fenway Park,** Boston Red Sox, opened in 1912

2. **Wrigley Field,** Chicago Cubs, 1914

3. **Dodger Stadium,** Los Angeles Dodgers, 1962

4. **Angel Stadium of Anaheim,** Los Angeles Angels, 1966

5. **Oakland Alameda County Coliseum,** Oakland Athletics, 1968

Source: Major League Baseball

TOP 5 Halloween Costumes for Kids

They're creepy, they're kooky. They're sparkly, fancy, or spooky. Halloween costumes make the autumn holiday super fun for everyone. Here are the most popular costumes of the 2012 season.

1. **Princess**

2. **Batman**

3. **Spider-Man**

4. **Witch**

5. **Disney Princess**

TOP 5 Halloween Costumes for Pets

Some pet-lovers just can't resist getting their cats and dogs into the holiday spirit. Here are the most popular costumes for pets in 2012.

1. Pumpkin

2. Devil

3. Hot dog

4. Cat

5. Bee

Source: National Retail Federation

9

TOP 5 AMERICAN INDIAN TRIBES

In the last census, 2.5 million people identified themselves as belonging to a specific tribal group. These are the largest.

1. NAVAJO
308,013 members

2. CHEROKEE
285,476 members

GUESS WHAT? November is American-Indian and Alaska-Native Heritage Month.

3. SIOUX
131,048 members

4. CHIPPEWA
115,859 members

5. CHOCTAW
88,913 members

Source: U.S. Census Bureau

TOP 5 Deepest Lakes

1.

Lake Baikal

Siberia, Russia

5,369 feet (1,637m) deep

2.

Lake Tanganyika

Tanzania, Burundi, Congo, and Zambia

4,826 feet (1,471 m) deep

3.

Caspian Sea

Iran, Russia, Azerbaijan, Kazakhstan, and Turkmenistan

3,362 feet (1,025 m) deep

4.

Lake Vostok

Antarctica

At least 2,950 feet (900 m) deep

5.

Lake O'Higgins/ San Martín

Chile and Argentina

2,742 feet (836 m) deep

Source: National Park Service

Most-Photographed City Sights

TOP 5

Researchers studied 35 million Flickr photos to come up with this list of the spots the most people visited and photographed.

1. Empire State Building
New York, New York

2. Trafalgar Square
London, England

3. Union Square
San Francisco, California

4. Eiffel Tower
Paris, France

5. Hollywood Walk of Fame
Los Angeles, California

TOP 5 Most-Recycled Items

People in the United States create about 250 million tons (227 million metric tons) of trash every year, and recycle about one-third of it. See which items are most likely to be tossed in the recycling bin.

1. Auto batteries	2. Newspaper*	3. Steel cans	4. Yard trimmings	5. Aluminum cans
96.2%	71.6%	67%	57.5%	49.6%

*Directories and some advertising and printed mail are counted along with newspapers. Office paper and magazines are not.

Source: The U.S. Environmental Protection Agency; *Municipal Solid Waste Generation, Recycling, and Disposal in the United States, Facts and Figures for 2010*

SNOWIEST PLACES
in the United States

Here are the U.S. places with the highest average annual snowfall.

1. **Valdez, AK**
326.3 inches (828.8 cm)

2. **Mount Washington, NH**
281.2 inches (714.2 cm)

4. **Anchorage, AK**
218 inches (555 cm)

3. **Herman, MI**
219.6 inches (557.8 cm)

5. **Lemolo Lake, OR**
217.1 inches (551 cm)

Source: National
Oceanic and
Atmospheric
Administration
(NOAA)

BACKYARD BIRDS

Bird-watchers in North America spotted millions of birds during the 2013 Great Backyard Bird Count. In the four-day event, people tallied how many of each species they saw, and filled out online checklists. These birds were seen the most.

1.
NORTHERN CARDINAL
46,991 birds sighted

2.
DARK-EYED JUNCO
42,819 birds sighted

3.
MOURNING DOVE
41,384 birds sighted

4.
DOWNY WOODPECKER
34,980 birds sighted

5.
HOUSE FINCH
32,476 birds sighted

Source : Great Backyard Bird Count; birdsource.org

TOP 5 BANANA EXPORTERS

These countries send the most bananas to
other nations around the world.

1. ECUADOR: 5,130,047 tons (4,653,900 metric tons) per year

2. PHILIPPINES: 2,099,572 tons (1,904,700 metric tons) per year

3. COSTA RICA: 1,755,651 tons (1,592,700 metric tons) per year

4. COLOMBIA: 1,651,703 tons (1,498,400 metric tons) per year

5. GUATEMALA: 1,245,061 tons (1,129,500 metric tons) per year

GUESS WHAT?
Americans go bananas
for bananas. On
average, an American
eats 27 pounds (12 kg)
in a year.

Source: Food and Agriculture Organization of the United Nations

TOP 5 CIVIL WAR BATTLE STATES

Historians say 384 big battles were fought during the Civil War. The South was especially hard-hit. These states had the most battles.

1. Virginia: 123 battles

2. Tennessee: 38 battles

TIE 3. Missouri: 27 battles
Georgia:

4. Louisiana: 23 battles

5. North Carolina: 20 battles

GUESS WHAT?
Civil War fighting took place in 25 U.S. states and territories, as well as in Washington, D.C.

Source: National Park Service

TOP$ \mathbf{5}$ Places Below Sea Level

The shore of the Dead Sea is the Earth's lowest point on dry land.
Here's the lowdown on the other low spots on the planet.

Source: U.S. Geological Survey

1. Dead Sea, Jordan and Israel
1,335 feet (407 m) below sea level

2. Lake Assal, Djibouti
505 feet (154 m) below sea level

3. **Turpan Depression, China**
499 feet (152 m) below sea level

4. **Qattara Depression, Egypt** TIE
Karagiye Depression, Kazakhstan
433 feet (132 m) below sea level

5. **Danakil Depression, Ethiopia**
394 feet (120 m) below sea level

TOP 5 Tea Drinkers

Nearly 80% of the people in the United Kingdom drink tea daily. Only water is more popular! Check out the nations where people drink the most tea.

1. Kuwait	**2.** Ireland	**3.** Afghanistan	**4.** Turkey	**5.** U.K.
6.44 pounds (2.9 kg) per person per year	4.8 pounds (2.2 kg) per person per year	4.54 pounds (2.1 kg) per person per year	4.39 pounds (2 kg) per person per year	4.23 pounds (1.9 kg) per person per year

GUESS WHAT? In 2012, people in the U.S. drank more than 66.5 billion servings of tea. About 84% of those servings were black tea (such as Earl Grey, Lady Grey, English breakfast, and Darjeeling black tea). Cups of green tea made up about 16% of the servings.

Source: Tea Council of the USA, Inc.; based on apparent consumption from 2009 to 2011

22

TOP 5

Largest Sea Turtles

Meet the world's largest sea turtles.

GUESS WHAT? Not all sea turtles have hard shells.

1. Leatherback turtle
3 to 6 feet long and up to 2,000 pounds
(1 to 2 m; 907 kg)

2. Green turtle
3 to 4 feet long and up to 500 pounds
(1 to 1.2 m; 227 kg)

3. Loggerhead turtle
2 to 3 feet long and up to 400 pounds
(0.6 to 1 m; 181 kg)

4. Flatback turtle
2.5 to 3 feet long and up to 200 pounds
(0.8 to 1 m; 91 kg)

5. Hawksbill turtle
2.5 to 3 feet long and up to 175 pounds
(0.8 to 1 m; 79 kg)

Source: The Marine Turtle Specialist Group

Gold-Producing Countries

China produces more than 350 tons (318 metric tons) of gold a year. That's about one-eighth of the world's gold. These countries produced the most gold in 2011.

1. **China**
355 tons
(322 metric tons)

2. **Australia**
270 tons
(245 metric tons)

3. **United States**
237 tons
(215 metric tons)

GUESS WHAT?
More gold is bought and sold in India than in any other country.

GUESS WHAT?
About 60% of all gold mined today is used for making jewelry.

Source: goldinvestingnews.com

4. **Russia**
200 tons
(181 metric tons)

5. **South Africa**
190 tons
(172 metric tons)

GUESS
WHAT?
Gold melts
at 1,947°F
(1,064°C).

TOP **5**

TURKEY-PRODUCING STATES

Americans usually eat more than 45 million turkeys on Thanksgiving Day. That's a little more than one bird for every seven people. Gobble, gobble! Here are the states that produced the most turkeys in 2012.

1.
Minnesota
46 million turkeys

2.
North Carolina
36 million turkeys

3.
Arkansas
29 million turkeys

4.
Missouri
17.5 million turkeys

5.
Virginia
17 million turkeys

Source: United States Department of Agriculture

TOP 5 LARGEST PLANETS

In 2006, scientists decided that tiny Pluto was not a planet. But these giants of our solar system don't have to worry about their place in space.

Source: NASA

1. Jupiter
88,732 miles
(142,800 km) across

2. Saturn
74,975 miles
(120,661 km) across

3. Uranus
31,763 miles
(51,118 km) across

4. Neptune
30,775 miles
(49,528 km) across

5. Earth
7,926 miles
(12,756 km) across

TOP 5 Heaviest Land Mammals

The lion may be king, but elephants are the heavy favorites.
Here is how other large land mammals measure up.

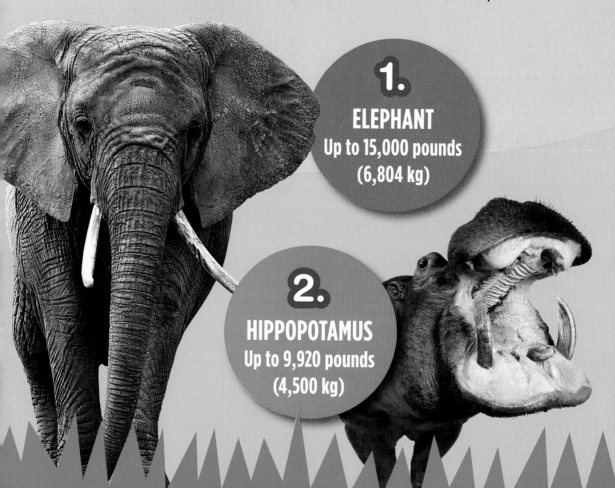

1.

ELEPHANT
Up to 15,000 pounds
(6,804 kg)

2.

HIPPOPOTAMUS
Up to 9,920 pounds
(4,500 kg)

4.
GIRAFFE
Up to 3,000 pounds
(1,361 kg)

5.
WATER BUFFALO
Up to 2,600 pounds
(1,179 kg)

3.
RHINOCEROS
Up to 5,000 pounds
(2,268 kg)

Source: The San Diego Zoo

Cereals with the Most Sugar

1. **Kellogg's Honey Smacks:** 56% sugar by weight

2. **Post Golden Crisp:** 52% sugar by weight

3. **Kellogg's Froot Loops Marshmallow:** 48% sugar by weight

4. **Quaker Oats Cap'n Crunch's Oops! All Berries:** 47% sugar by weight

5. **Quaker Oats Original Cap'n Crunch:** 44% sugar by weight

Source: Environmental Working Group

TOP 5 Wind-Energy Generators

China leads the world in total energy use. It also generates more energy from wind than any other country. Megawatts are used to measure power. The largest nuclear power plant in the United States produces 3,937 megawatts a year. Here are the nations that produce the most energy using wind turbines.

Source: Global Wind Energy Council, 2012

1. **China**
   75,564 megawatts

2. **United States**
   60,007 megawatts

3. **Germany**
   31,332 megawatts

4. **Spain**
   22,796 megawatts

5. **India**
   18,421 megawatts

1.
WILT CHAMBERLAIN
Philadelphia Warriors
March 2, 1962
100 points

TOP 5

NBA
Single-Game Scorers

Meet the players who have scored the most in a single game.

Source: nba.com

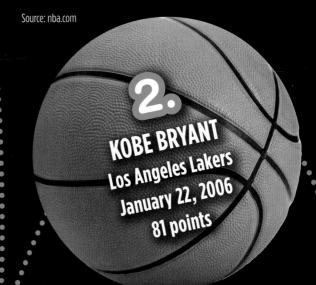

2.
KOBE BRYANT
Los Angeles Lakers
January 22, 2006
81 points

3.
WILT CHAMBERLAIN
Philadelphia Warriors
December 8, 1961
78 points

TIE 4.

WILT CHAMBERLAIN
Philadelphia Warriors
January 13, 1962
73 points

WILT CHAMBERLAIN
San Francisco Warriors
November 16, 1962
73 points

DAVID THOMPSON
Denver Nuggets
April 9, 1978
73 points

5.
WILT CHAMBERLAIN
San Francisco Warriors
November 3, 1962
72 points

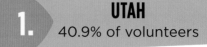

1. UTAH
40.9% of volunteers

U.S. States for Volunteering

2. IDAHO
38.8% of volunteers

3. IOWA
38.4% of volunteers

More than 60 million
Americans gave their time
in 2011. In which states are
volunteers most likely to
give more than 100 hours
of service per year?

4. MINNESOTA
38.0% of volunteers

5. SOUTH DAKOTA
36.8% of volunteers

Source: Corporation for National and Community Service

Most Popular Instruments

Whether electric or acoustic, many Americans go gaga over guitars. These are the instruments Americans spent the most money on in 2011.

Source: National Association of Music Merchants, 2011

1.
ACOUSTIC GUITARS
$483 million

5.
BRASS
$196 million

2.
ELECTRIC GUITARS
$452 million

4.
WOODWINDS
$268 million

3.
PIANOS
$291 million

TORNADO STATES

About 1,000 twisters hit the United States each year. Many are in an area called Tornado Alley. The map shows about how many storms strike the top tornado states yearly.

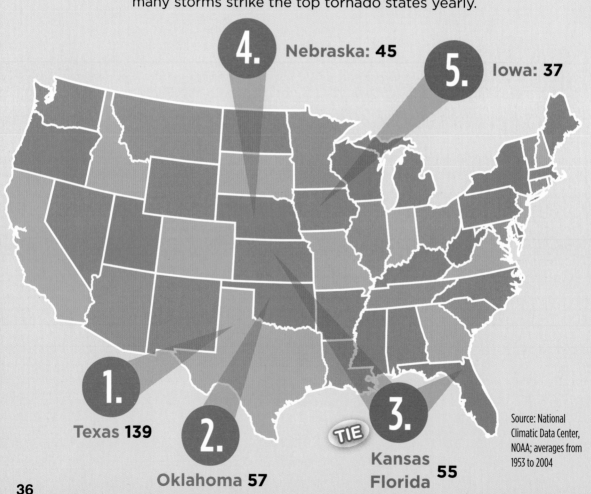

4. Nebraska: **45**

5. Iowa: **37**

1. Texas **139**

2. Oklahoma **57**

3. TIE Kansas **55** Florida

Source: National Climatic Data Center, NOAA; averages from 1953 to 2004

ICE-CREAM FLAVORS

I scream, you scream, we all scream for ice cream! Which flavor do you like best? When a large group of Americans were asked to name their favorite ice-cream flavor, these tasty flavors came out on top.

1. Vanilla 19%

2. Chocolate 11%

3. Cookies and cream 4%

4. French vanilla 3%

5. Chocolate chip 2.8%

GUESS WHAT?
Vanilla flavoring comes from pods that are the fruit of a particular type of flower, the vanilla orchid. Growing and harvesting vanilla is a difficult process, so the flavoring is quite expensive.

Source: The NPD Group

TOP 5 MOST-SEARCHED-FOR DICTIONARY WORDS

Do you know what *pretentious* means? It's the word most often searched for at Merriam-Webster's website. Here are the most-searched-for words.

1. **pretentious** (prih-*ten*-shus) *adjective:* trying to appear very important or valuable; exaggerating one's importance or skills

2. **ubiquitous** (yoo-*bik*-wih-tus) *adjective:* existing or being everywhere at the same time; widespread

3. **love** (luv) *noun:* a feeling of warm attachment, affection, or devotion for someone or something

4. **cynical** (*sin*-ih-kul) *adjective:* not trusting of human nature and motives

5. **apathetic** (ap-uh-*thet*-ik) *adjective:* having little or no interest or emotion; indifferent

Source: merriam-webster.com

TOP 5 CAT NAMES

Is there a special kitty in your family? Did you spend weeks coming up with the perfect name? Or did you know she was a Bella from her first meow? Here are the top cat names in the country.

1. **Bella**
2. **Max**
3. **Chloe**
4. **Oliver**
5. **Lucy**

Source: Veterinary Pet Insurance Company

TOP 5 Highest-Paid Women in Entertainment

There are countless hard-working, successful women in show business. But which female entertainers are worth the most money? Take a look.

1. OPRAH WINFREY $165 million

2. BRITNEY SPEARS $58 million

3. TAYLOR SWIFT $57 million

TIE 4. ELLEN DEGENERES
RIHANNA $53 million

TIE 5. LADY GAGA $52 million
JENNIFER LOPEZ

Source: forbes.com, 2012

Most Populous Nations

By 2026, there will be more people in India than in any other country. Here's how India ranks in 2013.

1. CHINA: 1.3 BILLION PEOPLE

2. INDIA: 1.2 BILLION PEOPLE

3. UNITED STATES: 317 MILLION PEOPLE

4. INDONESIA: 251 MILLION PEOPLE

5. BRAZIL: 201 MILLION PEOPLE

Sources: U.S. Census Bureau; CIA World Factbook

TOP 5 COUNTRIES FOR MATH

Every four years, fourth-grade students around the world are tested on their knowledge of math. Each country is graded on the same scale. Here are the highest scorers of 2012. The United States ranked 11th.

1. SINGAPORE 606

2. SOUTH KOREA 605

3. HONG KONG* 602

4. TAIWAN 591

5. JAPAN 585

*Hong Kong is a special administrative region of China that has a high degree of independence.
Source: National Center for Education Statistics

Countries for U.S. Tourists

Each year, millions of Americans flock to our sunny southern neighbor, Mexico. Here are the nations Americans visited the most in 2011.

1. **Mexico:** 20,084,000 U.S. travelers

2. **Canada:** 11,595,000 U.S. travelers

3. **United Kingdom:** 2,405,000 U.S. travelers

4. **France:** 1,756,000 U.S. travelers

5. **Italy:** 1,702,000 U.S. travelers

Source: ITA Office of Travel and Tourism Industries

TOP 5 **Valentine's Day Gifts**

Americans spend billions of dollars to celebrate Valentine's Day. What do they buy?

1.
JEWELRY
$4.1 billion

2.
EVENING OUT
$3.5 billion

3.
FLOWERS
$1.8 billion

4.
CANDY
$1.5 billion

5.
CLOTHING
$1.4 billion

44

Source: National Retail Federation, 2012

TOP 5 GREATEST BOOKS FOR KIDS

School Library Journal held a poll in 2012, asking readers about their favorite novels for 9-to-12-year-olds. Based on the results, *SLJ* created its list of the Top 100 Children's Novels for the 21st century. Below are the big winners.

1.
Charlotte's Web
by E.B. White

2.
A Wrinkle in Time
by Madeleine L'Engle

3.
Harry Potter and the Sorcerer's Stone
by J.K. Rowling

4.
The Giver
by Lois Lowry

5.
The Lion, the Witch, and the Wardrobe
by C.S. Lewis

Source: *School Library Journal*

TOP 5
Tallest Mountains

Earth's highest mountains are in the Himalayan system, which stretches across five countries and includes several ranges.

Source: *Merriam-Webster's Geographical Dictionary*, Third Edition

1.
EVEREST
NEPAL/CHINA
29,035 feet (8,850 m)

2.
K2
PAKISTAN/CHINA
28,250 feet (8,611 m)

3.
KANCHENJUNGA
NEPAL/INDIA
28,169 feet
(8,586 m)

4.
LHOTSE
NEPAL/CHINA
27,923 feet
(8,511 m)

5.
MAKALU
NEPAL/CHINA
27,824 feet
(8,481 m)

TOP 5 Trade Partners

The United States trades with countries all over the world. It sells, or exports, some products, and buys, or imports, others. Canada is this country's largest trade partner. Here are the countries that the U.S. traded with the most in 2012.

1.
CANADA
$616.7 billion in goods

2.
CHINA
$536.2 billion in goods

3.
MEXICO
$494 billion in goods

4.
JAPAN
$216.4 billion in goods

5.
GERMANY
$157.3 billion in goods

Source: U.S. Census Bureau, Foreign Trade Statistics Division

TOP 5 Highest-Grossing Kids Movies of All Time

These kid-friendly films have made the most
money in the United States.

1. *Star Wars: Episode I—The Phantom Menace* — $474,544,677

2. *Star Wars** — $460,998,007

3. *Shrek 2* — $441,226,247

4. *E.T. the Extra-Terrestrial* — $435,110,554

5. *The Lion King* — $422,783,777

*Original title; also known as *Stars Wars: Episode IV—A New Hope*
Source: IMDB.com. This list includes only films rated G or PG and is based on U.S. sales to May 2013.

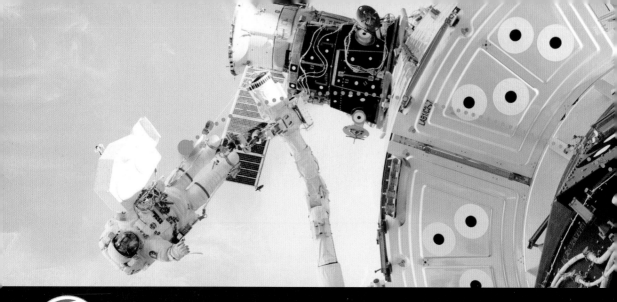

⑤ TOP LONGEST SPACEWALKS

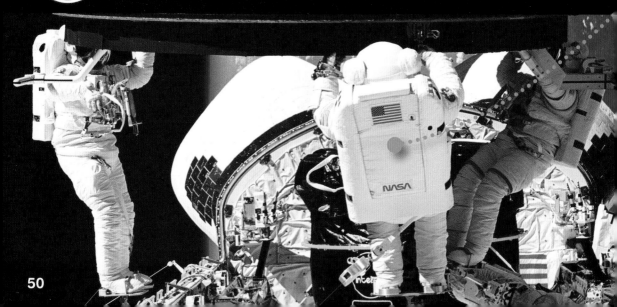

U.S. astronauts have been on more than 100 spacewalks. Here are the longest-ever spacewalks, and the U.S. astronauts who took them.

Source: Compiled by TIME FOR KIDS

ASTRONAUTS	DATE	HOURS	MINUTES
1. James Voss, Susan Helms	March 10–11, 2001	8	56
2. Thomas D. Akers, Richard J. Hieb, Pierre J. Thuot	May 13, 1992	8	29
3. John M. Grunsfeld, Steven L. Smith	December 22, 1999	8	15
4. C. Michael Foale, Claude Nicollier	December 23, 1999	8	10
5. John M. Grunsfeld, Steven L. Smith	December 24, 1999	8	8

TOP 5 YOUNGEST PRESIDENTS

According to the Constitution, the President must be at least 35 years old. Theodore Roosevelt is the youngest person to have become President. He succeeded William McKinley, who was assassinated. Here are the youngest and oldest Presidents and their ages when they took office.

1. Theodore Roosevelt
42 years, 322 days

2. John F. Kennedy
43 years, 236 days

Source: whitehouse.gov

3. Bill Clinton
46 years, 149 days

4. Ulysses S. Grant
46 years, 311 days

5. Barack Obama
47 years, 169 days

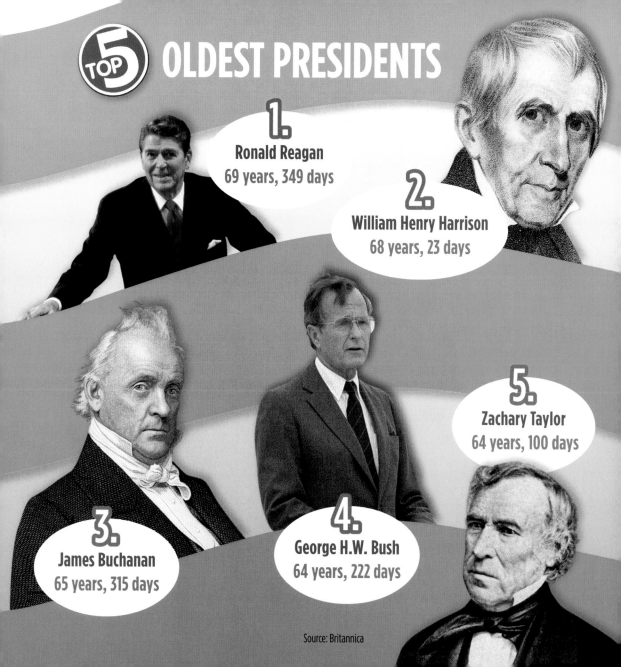

TOP 5 OLDEST PRESIDENTS

1.
Ronald Reagan
69 years, 349 days

2.
William Henry Harrison
68 years, 23 days

3.
James Buchanan
65 years, 315 days

4.
George H.W. Bush
64 years, 222 days

5.
Zachary Taylor
64 years, 100 days

Source: Britannica

TOP 5 COLLEGE BASKETBALL CHAMPIONS

These NCAA (National Collegiate Athletic Association) men's teams have won the most championships through 2013.

1. U.C.L.A.
11 CHAMPIONSHIPS

4. DUKE
4 CHAMPIONSHIPS

2. KENTUCKY
8 CHAMPIONSHIPS

5. *TIE* LOUISVILLE CONNECTICUT
3 CHAMPIONSHIPS

3. *TIE* NORTH CAROLINA INDIANA
5 CHAMPIONSHIPS

Source: NCAA

TOP 5

Tallest Buildings

Source: EMPORIS

1.
Burj Khalifa in Dubai, United Arab Emirates

2,717 feet (830 m)

2.
Abraj Al-Bait Towers in Mecca, Saudi Arabia

1,971 feet (601 m)

3.
One World Trade Center in New York City

1,776 feet (541 m)

4.
Taipei 101 in Taipei, Taiwan

1,670 feet (509 m)

5.
Shanghai World Financial Center in Shanghai, China

1,614 feet (492 m)

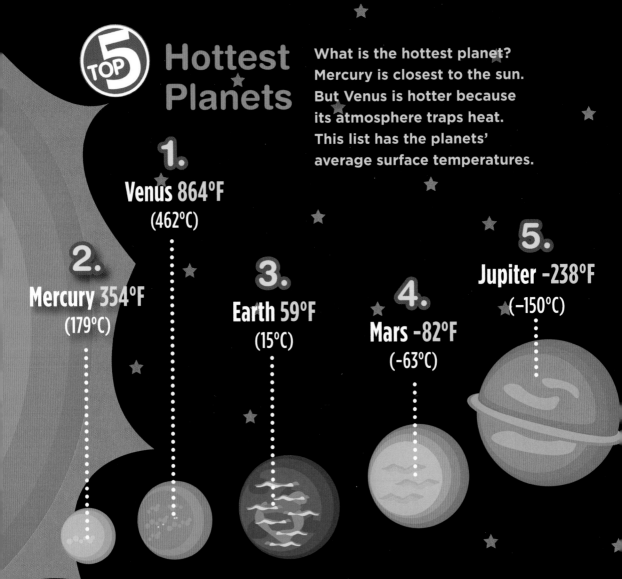

TOP 5 Hottest Planets

What is the hottest planet? Mercury is closest to the sun. But Venus is hotter because its atmosphere traps heat. This list has the planets' average surface temperatures.

1.
Venus 864°F
(462°C)

2.
Mercury 354°F
(179°C)

3.
Earth 59°F
(15°C)

4.
Mars -82°F
(-63°C)

5.
Jupiter -238°F
(-150°C)

Source: NASA

TOP 5 Friendliest Countries

Where would you want to live?
Americans living in more than 100 countries
were asked their opinions. They voted on
where it is easiest to befriend locals and
learn the language and culture.

1. **Cayman Islands**
2. **Australia**
3. **United Kingdom**
4. **Canada**
5. **New Zealand**

GUESS WHAT?
The Cayman Islands is made up of three islands: Grand Cayman, Cayman Brac, and Little Cayman. The tropical destination is very popular with divers.

Sources: Forbes; HSBC's Expat Explorer Survey, 2012

TOP 5 Biggest Spiders

Do spiders give you chills? Take a look at the biggest spiders in the world, measured by leg span.

1. Huntsman spider: **11.8 inches** (30 cm)

2. Brazilian salmon-pink spider: **10.6 inches** (26.9 cm)

3. Brazilian giant tawny spider: 10.2 inches (25.9 cm)

4. Goliath birdeater: 10 inches (25.4 cm)

5. Wolf spider: 10 inches (25.4 cm)

Source: scienceray.com

TOP 5 LARGEST LIBRARIES

The Library of Congress, in Washington, D.C., has the largest collection of any U.S. library. See how other big U.S. libraries stack up.

Source: American Library Association

1. Library of Congress
33,515,702 volumes

2. Boston Public Library
24,079,520 volumes

3. New York Public Library
16,640,294 volumes

4. Harvard University
16,557,002 volumes

5. University of Illinois at Urbana–Champaign
12,780,067 volumes

TOP 5 ELEMENTS FOUND IN THE HUMAN BODY

Water is made up of hydrogen and oxygen. So it's not surprising that those elements are two of the most common in the human body. Here are the top elements found in an average-size adult.

1. **Oxygen:** 65% of body mass

2. **Carbon:** 18% of body mass

3. **Hydrogen:** 10% of body mass

4. **Nitrogen:** 3% of body mass

5. **Calcium:** 1.5% of body mass

Source: oxygen-review.com

FAVORITE PIES FOR THE HOLIDAYS

What's more American than apple pie? Nothing! Crisco and the American Pie Council asked people what pie they eat during the holidays. Apple pie beat all the rest.

2. Pumpkin 13%

3. Pecan 12%

4. Banana cream 10%

1. Apple 19%

5. Cherry 9%

Other 37%

Source: Crisco and the American Pie Council

Chocolate-Loving Countries

On average, Americans spent $58 per person on chocolate in 2011. It may seem like a lot of money, but it's nothing compared to Norway. Here are the countries that spent the most per person, on average, on the sweet treat.

1.

Norway
$209

2.

Ireland
$182

3.

Switzerland
$172

4.

United Kingdom
$150

5.

Austria
$112

Source: Euromonitor International

TOP 5 MOST POPULOUS CITIES

Here are the urban areas with the largest populations.

1. **Tokyo, Japan** 37.22 million

2. **Delhi, India** 22.65 million

3. **Mexico City, Mexico** 20.45 million

4. **New York–Newark, United States*** 20.35 million

5. **Shanghai, China** 20.21 million

*The population is for a larger area that includes more than one city.

Source: United Nations, World Urbanization Prospects, 2011

TOP 5 Longest Rivers

1. **Nile** (Africa) 4,132 miles (6,650 km)

2. **Amazon** (South America) 4,000 miles (6,437 km)

3. **Chang/Yangtze** (Asia) 3,915 miles (6,301 km)

4. **Mississippi** (North America) 3,710 miles (5,971 km)

5. **Yenisei** (Asia) 3,442 miles (5,539 km)

Source: britannica.com

TOP 5

STATES FOR CYBER KIDS

The number of students who attend school online in the United States is on the rise. Here are the states that had the most students attending full-time online schools, according to a recent study.

Source: Keeping Pace with K–12 Online Learning: An Annual Review of Policy and Practice, 2010

Ohio	Arizona	Pennsylvania	Colorado	Washington
31,852 students	30,338 students	24,603 students	13,093 students	13,000 students
1.	2.	3.	4.	5.

TOP 5 **Biggest Droughts in the United States**

These are the months on record when the largest portions of the United States were in drought.

Source: National Climatic Data Center

1.
JULY 1934:
79.9% in drought

2.
DECEMBER 1939:
62.1% in drought

3.
JULY 1954:
60.4% in drought

4.
DECEMBER 1956:
57.6% in drought

5.
JULY 2012:
57.2% in drought

TOP 5 FASTEST ANIMAL SPEEDS

1. **CHEETAH** 70 miles (113 km) per hour

2. **PRONGHORN** 61 miles (98 km) per hour

3. **THOMSON'S GAZELLE, WILDEBEEST, AND LION** TIE 50 miles (80 km) per hour

4. **QUARTER HORSE** 48 miles (77 km) per hour

5. **ELK** 45 miles (72 km) per hour

The animal kingdom has many swift runners. Some creatures can move faster than a speeding car. In the list of the five fastest land animals, there is a three-way tie for third place.

Oldest National Parks

Source: nps.gov

GUESS WHAT?
The National Park Service is responsible for more than 400 land areas in the United States. This includes more than 84 million acres (339,936 sq km) of land and 17,000 miles (27,359 km) of trails.

1.

Founded
March 1, 1872

Yellowstone National Park
(Wyoming, Montana, Idaho)

2.

Founded
September 25, 1890

Sequoia National Park
(California)

3.

TIE

Founded
October 1, 1890

**General Grant
National Park***
AND
**Yosemite
National Park**
(Both in California)

*Name changed to
Kings Canyon National Park in 1940

4.

Founded
March 2, 1899

**Mount Rainier
National Park**
(Washington)

5.

Founded
May 22, 1902

**Crater Lake
National Park**
(Oregon)

TOP 5 SUGAR CULPRITS

Most people eat more sugar than they realize. The sweet stuff is added to many foods and drinks. Here are the things we eat and drink that add the most sugar to our diet.

Source: American Heart Association

1. Soft drinks 33%

2. Candy 16%

3. Cakes, cookies, and pies 13%

4. Fruit drinks 10%

5. Dairy desserts 9%

6. Other: 19%

GUESS WHAT?
There are 1.4 ounces (41 g) of sugar in 12 ounces (355 ml) of Coca-Cola Classic. That's 10 teaspoons of sugar in a single can!

COLDEST INAUGURATIONS

Source: NOAA; based on the temperature at noon

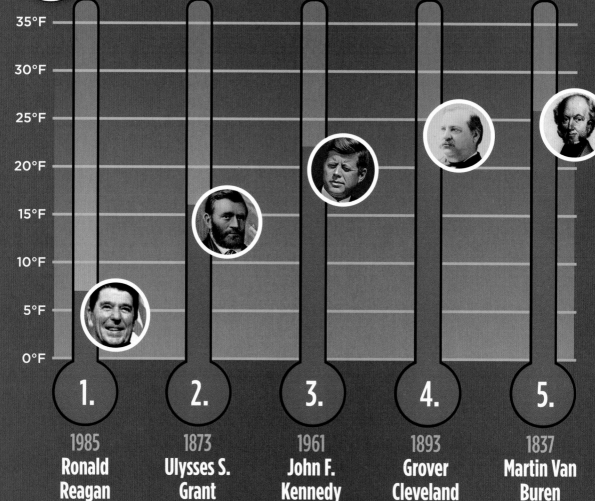

35°F				
30°F				
25°F				
20°F				
15°F				
10°F				
5°F				
0°F				

1.	2.	3.	4.	5.
1985	1873	1961	1893	1837
Ronald Reagan	**Ulysses S. Grant**	**John F. Kennedy**	**Grover Cleveland**	**Martin Van Buren**
7°F (-14°C)	16°F (-9°C)	22°F (-6°C)	25°F (-4°C)	26°F (-3°C)

TOP 5 Peppermint Producers

Green tea flavored with fresh mint is Morocco's national drink. The country grows more peppermint than any other country. See which other nations are top peppermint producers.

1. Morocco
79,234 tons (71,880 metric tons)

2. Argentina
7,826 tons (7,100 metric tons)

3. Spain
661 tons (600 metric tons)

4. Bulgaria
392 tons (356 metric tons)

5. Georgia
33 tons (30 metric tons)

Source: Food and Agriculture Organization of the United Nations, 2011

TOP 5 LONGEST BIRD

For decades, scientists believed the Arctic tern migrated farther than any bird. Which bird bumped the tern from the top spot? Look at the list.

1. Sooty shearwater
40,000 miles (64,374 km) traveled per year

2. Arctic tern
24,000 miles (38,624 km) traveled per year

3. Bar-tailed godwit
20,000 miles (32,187 km) traveled per year

4. Common nighthawk
14,000 miles (22,531 km) traveled per year

5. Blackpoll warbler
10,000 miles (16,093 km) traveled per year

MIGRATIONS

Source: Laura Erickson, Science Editor, Cornell Lab of Ornithology

TOP 5 Hispanic Places of Origin

About 52 million Hispanic people live in the United States. They trace their origins to many Spanish-speaking places. Here are the top countries, as of 2010.

1.

MEXICO
31,798,258 people

2.

PUERTO RICO
4,623,716 people

3.

CUBA
1,785,547 people

4.

EL SALVADOR
1,648,968 people

5.

DOMINICAN REPUBLIC
1,414,703 people

Source: U.S. Census Bureau

TOP 5 QUALITIES OF A GREAT TEACHER

KidsHealth asked more than 6,000 kids, "What is the Number 1 quality that makes a teacher great?" Here are their answers.

1.
Explains things well and is interesting
32%

2.
Patient and answers questions
25%

3.
Funny and has a great personality
24%

4.
Interested in students' opinions
8%

5.
Tech savvy
5%

Other 6%

Source: kidshealth.org

81

TOP 5

Best Countries for Women

In 2010, a business group scored 134 countries on how close they are to giving equal opportunities to men and women. The United States ranked 19th, with a 74% score. Here are the top countries for women.

Source: World Economic Forum

1. Iceland: **85%**
2. Norway: **84%**
3. Finland: **83%**
4. Sweden: **80%**
5. New Zealand: **78%**

Hurricane States

Hurricanes are a dangerous force of nature. Coastal states experience them most often. Here are the U.S. states that had the most hurricanes from 1851 to 2010.

1. Florida 114 hurricanes

2. Texas 64 hurricanes

3. Louisiana 57 hurricanes

4. North Carolina 51 hurricanes

5. South Carolina 30 hurricanes

Source: NOAA

Countries with the Biggest Tropical Rain Forests

BRAZIL

1,800,000 square miles
(4,661,979 square km)

2.

DEMOCRATIC REPUBLIC OF THE CONGO

683,400 square miles
(1,769,997 square km)

3.
INDONESIA
490,349 square miles
(1,269,998 square km)

4.
PERU
289,576 square miles
(749,998 square km)

5.
COLOMBIA
258,688 square miles
(669,999 square km)

Source: World Resources Institute

TOP 5 MOST POPULAR

1. DOGS
46.3 million U.S. households

2. CATS
38.9 million U.S. households

PETS

Cats are chasing dogs in this race! More homes in the United States have a dog than any other pet. Here are the top pet picks in the U.S.

GUESS WHAT?
If cared for properly, a goldfish can live up to 20 years and grow up to 1 foot (30 cm) long.

3. FISH
12.6 million U.S. households

4. BIRDS
5.7 million U.S. households

5. SMALL ANIMALS
5 million U.S. households

Source: APPA'S 2011–2012 National Pet Owners Survey

TOP 5 TECH ITEMS FOR KIDS

A research group asked U.S. kids ages 6 to 12 about the gadgets on their wish lists. Nearly half of the children surveyed wanted an iPad. Here are the most-wanted items.

1.
iPad
48%

2.
Nintendo Wii U
39%

TIE **3.**

iPod Touch

iPad Mini

36%

4.

iPhone

33%

TIE **5.**

Computer

Kinect For Xbox 360

31%

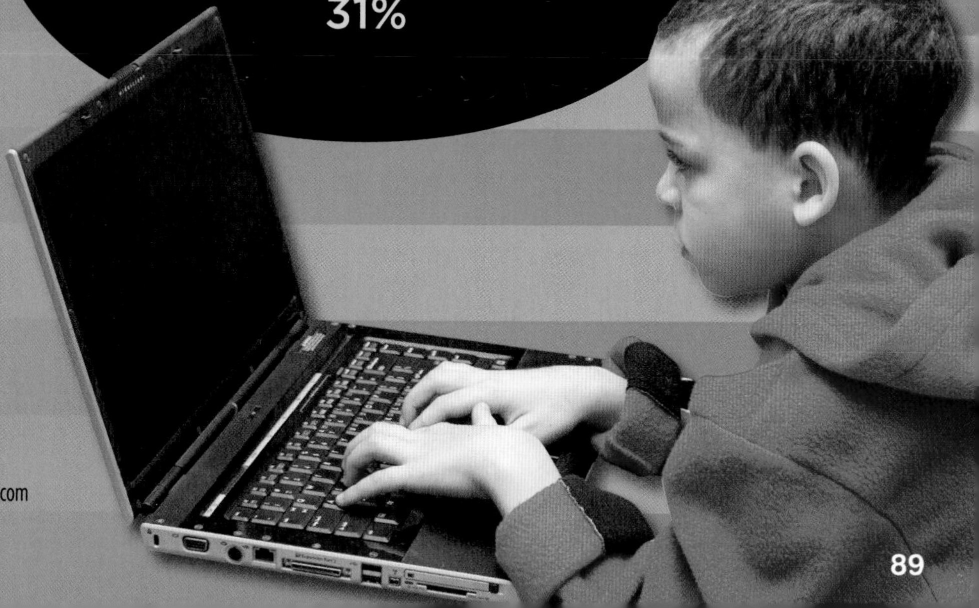

Source: nielsen.com

LARGEST CONTINENTS

1.
Asia

17,139,445 square miles
(44,390,959 square km)

2.
Africa

11,677,239 square miles
(30,243,910 square km)

3.
North America

9,361,791 square miles
(24,246,927 square km)

4.
South America

6,880,706 square miles
(17,820,947 square km)

GUESS WHAT?
Antarctica is the only continent with no permanent human residents.

5.
Antarctica

5,500,000 square miles
(14,244,935 square km)

Source: *Merriam-Webster's Geographical Dictionary*, Third Edition

All-Time Favorite Toys

About 20,000 people voted for the most popular toys of the past 100 years. These toys came out on top.

Source: The Children's Museum of Indianapolis

1. G.I. Joe
1,840 votes

2. Transformers
1,104 votes

3. LEGO
844 votes

4. Barbie
842 votes

5. View-Master
701 votes

TOP 5 CINNAMON GROWERS

Cinnamon is the peeled, dried bark of a tree.

GUESS WHAT?
Indonesia's Molucca Islands were once known as the Spice Islands.

1. INDONESIA
66,139 tons (60,000 metric tons) per year

2. CHINA
60,627 tons (55,000 metric tons) per year

3. SRI LANKA
14,727 tons (13,360 metric tons) per year

4. VIETNAM
13,779 tons (12,500 metric tons) per year

5. MADAGASCAR
1,819 tons (1,650 metric tons) per year

Source: FAOSTAT

TOP 5 VETERAN WARS

This chart shows the wars served by the most U.S. forces.

World War II (1941–1945)
16,112,566 U.S. service members
 1.

Vietnam War (1964–1975)
8,744,000 U.S. service members
 2.

Korean War (1950–1953)
5,720,000 U.S. service members
 3.

World War I (1917–1918)
4,734,991 U.S. service members
4.

Desert Shield/Desert Storm (1990–1991)
2,322,000 service members
 5.

Source: U.S. Department of Veterans Affairs

1. Spain

252 million gallons
(953 million liters)

TOP 5

Olive Oil Producers

Greeks consume more olive oil per person per year than anyone else in the world, but Spain is the world's top producer.

2. Italy

151 million gallons
(570 million liters)

Source: International Olive Oil Council

GUESS WHAT?
As part of a healthful diet, olive oil is believed to reduce the risk of heart disease and cancer and the effects of aging.

GUESS WHAT?
Olive oil is obtained from the fruit of the olive tree. It is used in cooking, cosmetics, soaps, and even as fuel for oil lamps.

3.
Greece
108 million gallons
(407 million liters)

4.
Tunisia
68 million gallons
(256 million liters)

5.
Syria
61 million gallons
(230 million liters)

TOP **5** BIGGEST CATS

1. TIGER 673 pounds (305 kg)

2. LION 550 pounds (249 kg)

Here are the heavyweight champs of the cat kingdom, by the top weight of the males.

3. JAGUAR 264 pounds (120 kg)

4. PUMA 227 pounds (103 kg)

5. LEOPARD 198 pounds (90 kg)

Source: Walker's Mammals of the World

TOP 5 TESTERS

The newspaper *Education Week* grades each U.S. state's testing program. In 2013, more than 20 states received A grades for giving students high-quality exams. Here are the scores of the top states.

1. **Indiana** 97.8

2. **Louisiana** 97.2

3. **West Virginia** 96.7

4. **Ohio** 96.1

5. **Florida** 95

Source: Quality Counts 2013 Report (Standards, Assessment, and Accountability)

APPLE-GROWING STATES

1. Washington	2. New York	3. Michigan	4. Pennsylvania	5. California
132 million bushels	30 million bushels	14 million bushels	12 million bushels	7 million bushels

Source: U.S. Apple Association

Longest Bridges

These amazing structures help people travel over swamps and bodies of water. Here are the longest bridges made for cars and drivers.

Source: *USA Today*

1. **Lake Pontchartrain Causeway, United States**
126,122 feet (38,442 m)

2. **Manchac Swamp Bridge, United States**
120,440 feet (36,710 m)

3. **Hangzhou Bay Bridge, China**
117,037 feet (35,673 m)

4. **Runyang Bridge, China**
116,990 feet (35,660 m)

5. **Donghai Bridge, China**
106,600 feet (32,500 m)

TOP 5

TALLEST PRESIDENTS

1. **ABRAHAM LINCOLN**
6 feet 4 inches (193 cm)

2. **LYNDON B. JOHNSON**
6 feet 3 inches (190.5 cm)

3. **THOMAS JEFFERSON**
6 feet 2.5 inches (189 cm)

4. **GEORGE H.W. BUSH**
TIE **BILL CLINTON**
FRANKLIN D. ROOSEVELT
GEORGE WASHINGTON
CHESTER A. ARTHUR
6 feet 2 inches (188 cm)

5. **ANDREW JACKSON**
TIE **RONALD REAGAN**
BARACK OBAMA
6 feet 1 inch (185 cm)

Source: whitehouse.gov

LONGEST NIGHT'S · SLEEP

A study of people in 18 nations reveals that people in France average one hour more of sleep each night than do South Koreans. This graph compares the average night's rest for people in five countries.

Source: Organization for Economic Cooperation and Development

1.
FRANCE
8.8 hours

2.
UNITED STATES
8.6 hours

3.
MEXICO
8.4 hours

4.
GERMANY
8.2 hours

5.
SOUTH KOREA
7.8 hours

TOP 5 Tallest Mountains in the United States

The 16 tallest mountains in the United States are in Alaska. The state is home to 39 mountain ranges.

1. **Mt. McKinley:** 20,320 feet (6,194 m)

2. **Mt. St. Elias:** 18,008 feet (5,489 m)

3. **Mt. Foraker:** 17,400 feet (5,304 m)

4. **Mt. Bona:** 16,500 feet (5,029 m)

5. **Mt. Blackburn:** 16,390 feet (4,996 m)

GUESS WHAT? Mount McKinley, in Denali National Park, is the tallest mountain in North America.

Source: U.S. Geological Survey

TOP 5 DOG NAMES

Out of 485,000 insured pets, these were the top dog names of 2012.

1. **Bella** 5,660

2. **Bailey** 3,988

3. **Max** 3,958

4. **Lucy** 3,571

5. **Molly** 3,281

Source: Veterinary Pet Insurance Company

Nations with the Most School Hours

Here are the countries where students ages 9 to 11 spend the most time in school per year. The list does not include information about U.S. schools.

5.

TIE **ITALY**
LUXEMBOURG
924 hours per year

1.
CHILE
1,083 hours per year

4.
THE NETHERLANDS
940 hours per year

2.
ISRAEL
990 hours per year

3.
AUSTRALIA
984 hours per year

Source: Organization for Economic Cooperation and Development

BEST INVENTIONS

The Science Museum of London, in England, asked visitors to vote on which modern invention or discovery has made the greatest impact. Out of 48,152 votes, the X-ray machine got top honors.

Source: Science Museum of London

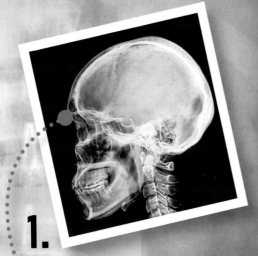

1.
X-ray machine
9,581 votes

2.
Penicillin
6,825 votes

3.

Structure of DNA (the chemical that carries the code for every living thing)

6,725 votes

4.

Apollo 10 capsule

4,649 votes

5.

V2 rocket engine

3,985 votes

TOP 5 Strongest Earthquakes

This list shows the largest earthquakes since 1900.

1. Chile, 1960 — 9.5 magnitude

2. Prince William Sound, Alaska, 1964 — 9.2 magnitude

3. Off the coast of northern Sumatra, 2004 — 9.1 magnitude

TIE
4. Near the coast of Honshu, Japan, 2011
Kamchatka Peninsula, Russia, 1952 — 9.0 magnitude

TIE
5. Offshore Bio-Bio, Chile, 2010
Off the coast of Ecuador, 1906 — 8.8 magnitude

Source: usgs.gov

LONGEST-RUNNING BROADWAY SHOWS

1.
Phantom of the Opera 10,527 performances*

2.
Cats 7,485 performances

3.
Chicago (Revival) 6,853 performances*

4.
Les Misérables 6,680 performances

5.
The Lion King 6,455 performances*

*Still running as of June 2013

Source: playbill.com, May 2013

TOP 5 Longest Land-Mammal Migrations

Some land mammals migrate in search of food or because of a change in weather. In Alaska, the caribous are always on the move. Here are the longest average round-trips. The numbers are based on animals living in the regions named.

1. Barren-ground caribou: 2,706 miles (4,355 km)
(Arctic Refuge, Alaska)

2. Wildebeest: 498 miles (801 km)
(Serengeti, Tanzania)

Source: Joel Berger/
Conservation Biology, 2004

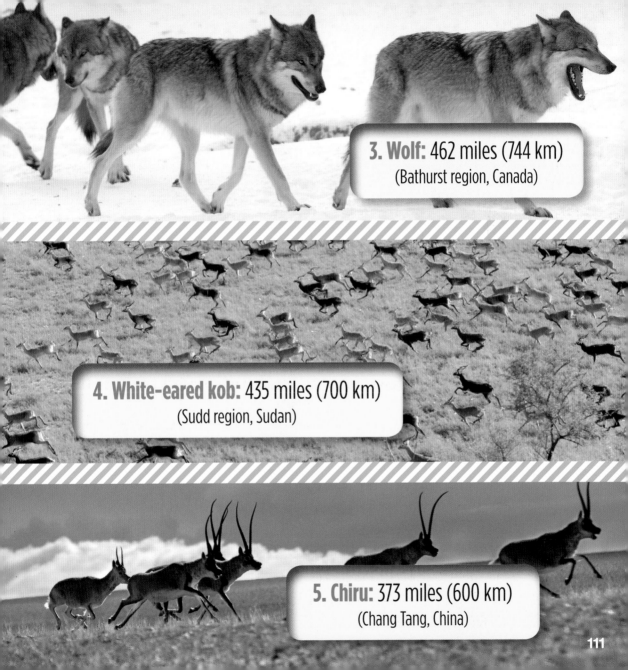

3. Wolf: 462 miles (744 km)
(Bathurst region, Canada)

4. White-eared kob: 435 miles (700 km)
(Sudd region, Sudan)

5. Chiru: 373 miles (600 km)
(Chang Tang, China)

TOP 5 Planets with the Most Moons

There are 146 known moons in our solar system.
Scientists have found other possible moons that have not yet been confirmed.

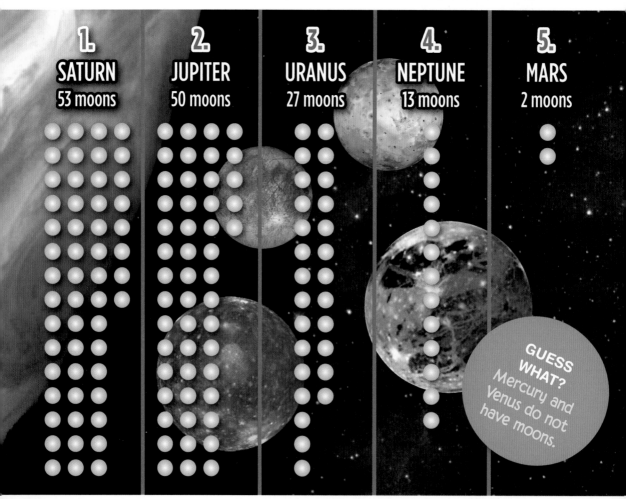

1.
SATURN
53 moons

2.
JUPITER
50 moons

3.
URANUS
27 moons

4.
NEPTUNE
13 moons

5.
MARS
2 moons

GUESS WHAT? Mercury and Venus do not have moons.

TOP 5 Most Popular Dog Breeds in the United States

Source: The American Kennel Club

1. Labrador retriever

2. German shepherd

3. Beagle

4. Golden retriever

5. Yorkshire terrier

GUESS WHAT?
The Labrador retriever has been the top dog in the U.S. for more than 20 years.

TOP 5 Longest Snakes

1. RETICULATED PYTHON
35 feet (10.7 m)

2. GREEN ANACONDA 28 feet (8.5 m)

3. INDIAN PYTHON 25 feet (7.6 m)

4. DIAMOND PYTHON 21 feet (6.4 m)

5. KING COBRA 19 feet (5.8 m)

Source: *Top 10 of Everything 2007*, Octopus Publishing Group Ltd.

TOP 5

NFL TEAMS

From 2003 to 2012, these teams won the most games.

Source: nfl.com

1.
New England Patriots
126 games

2.
Indianapolis Colts
112 games

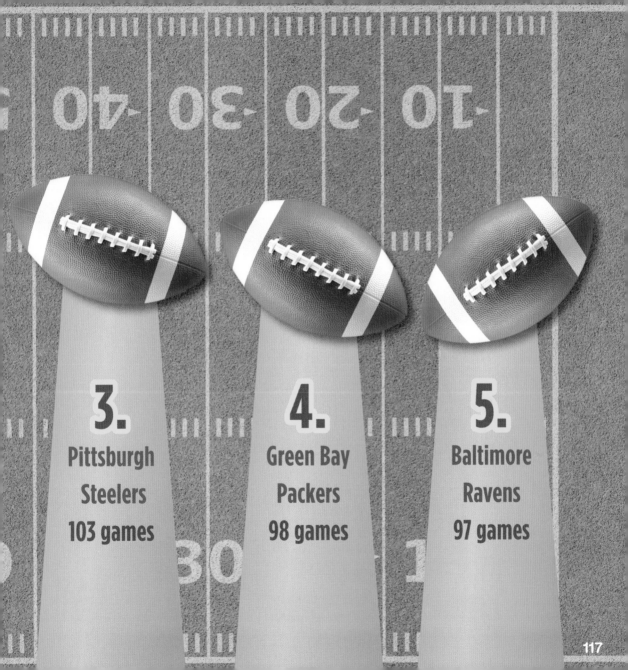

3.
Pittsburgh
Steelers
103 games

4.
Green Bay
Packers
98 games

5.
Baltimore
Ravens
97 games

MOST-PRODUCED PLAYS

Almost, Maine topped the list of full-length plays that were produced most often in high schools around the United States.

1. **Almost, Maine,** by John Cariani

2. **Twelve Angry Jurors,*** by Reginald Rose

3. **A Midsummer Night's Dream,** by William Shakespeare

4. **Our Town,** by Thornton Wilder

5. **You Can't Take It with You,** by George S. Kaufman and Moss Hart

*Includes productions under the title *Twelve Angry Men.*

Source: Educational Theatre Association, 2011–2012 Annual Play Survey

TOP 5 States for Green Technology

Where in the United States are people using eco-friendly vehicles, constructing green buildings, and generating electricity from renewable sources? A recent study looked at these factors and more to determine which U.S. states are leaders in clean, green technology. California took the top honors with a score of 91.7.

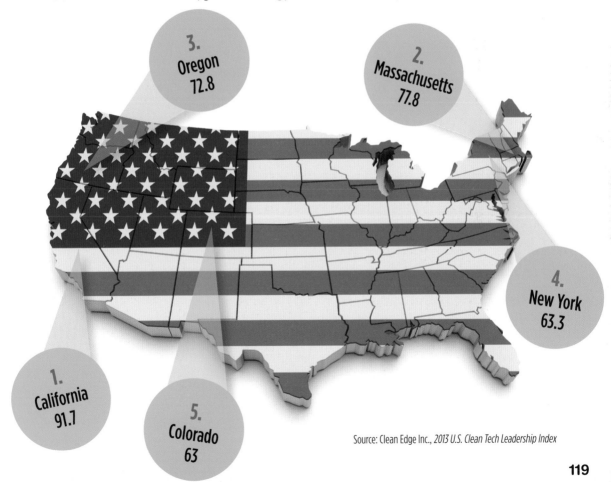

3.
Oregon
72.8

2.
Massachusetts
77.8

4.
New York
63.3

1.
California
91.7

5.
Colorado
63

Source: Clean Edge Inc., *2013 U.S. Clean Tech Leadership Index*

TOP 5 Actresses with the Most Academy Award Nominations

1. **Meryl Streep 17 nominations**

2. **Katharine Hepburn 12 nominations**

3. **Bette Davis 10 nominations**

4. **Geraldine Page 8 nominations**

TIE 5. **Ingrid Bergman**
   Jane Fonda   7 nominations
   Greer Garson

GUESS WHAT? Meryl Streep has won three Oscars.

TOP 5 Actors with the Most Academy Award Nominations

1. **Jack Nicholson** 12 nominations

2. **Laurence Olivier** 10 nominations

3. **Spencer Tracy**
TIE **Paul Newman** 9 nominations

4. **Marlon Brando**
TIE **Jack Lemmon**
   Peter O'Toole 8 nominations
   Al Pacino

5. **Richard Burton**
TIE **Robert De Niro** 7 nominations
   Dustin Hoffman

GUESS WHAT? Jack Nicholson has won three Oscars.

Source: The Academy of Motion Picture Arts and Sciences; as of June 2013

TOP 5 Voting States

On November 6, 2012, U.S. voters went to the polls to cast their votes for President Barack Obama or challenger Mitt Romney. Here are the states with the highest turnout rates among eligible voters.

1. **MINNESOTA** 75.7%

2. **WISCONSIN** 72.5%

3. **COLORADO** 70.3%

4. **NEW HAMPSHIRE** .. 70.1%

5. **IOWA** 69.9%

GUESS WHAT?
With 44.2% of its eligible citizens showing up at the polls, Hawaii had the lowest voter turnout in the 2012 presidential election.

GUESS WHAT?
In the 2008 presidential election, Minnesota and Wisconsin also topped the list of states with the highest voter turnout.

Source: U.S. Elections Project

1. United States

 **Toy-Buying Countries**

When it comes to toys, Americans aren't playing around! More money is spent on toys in the United States than in any other country. See where people spent the most money on toys in 2010.

Source: The NPD Group, Toy Markets Around the World Annual 2010

2. Japan

3. China

4. United Kingdom
TIE France

5. Germany

$22 billion $7 billion $6 billion $4 billion $3 billion

TOP 5 WARMEST JANUARYS

Here are the average temperatures
for the warmest Januarys on
record in the United States.

1. 2006 39.0°F (3.9°C)

2. 1954 37.3°F (2.9°C)

3. 1990 37.2°F (2.89°C)

4. 2012 36.3°F (2.4°C)

5. 1934 36.0°F (2.2°C)

Source: National Climatic Data Center

TOP 5 COFFEE-PRODUCING COUNTRIES

1.
BRAZIL
48,095,000 bags of coffee per year

5.
ETHIOPIA
7,450,000 bags of coffee per year

2.
VIETNAM
18,500,000 bags of coffee per year

4.
INDONESIA
8,500,000 bags of coffee per year

3.
COLOMBIA
9,200,000 bags of coffee per year

Source: International Coffee Organization, May 2011

TOP 5 DATED INVENTIONS

The gas-powered car is on its way out, according to a survey of 500 teens. Take a look at the inventions they say are headed for the trash heap.

1. Gas-powered car: 37%
2. Landline phone: 32%
3. Computer mouse: 21%
4. Other (includes books, DVDs, VCRs, and radios): 4%
5. Television: 3%

Source: Lemelson-MIT Invention Index

TOP 5 GOALS FOR GOOD HEALTH

TIME For Kids and KidsHealth questioned more than 10,000 kids about health. We asked kids what health goals they'd like an adult's help to achieve. This is what they said.

1.
Learning how to cook

4,450 kids

2.
Getting more exercise

3,280 kids

3.
Eating healthier foods

3,242 kids

4.
Learning how to play new sports

2,990 kids

5.
Losing weight

2,579 kids

Sources: KidsHealth and TIME For Kids

TOP 5 MOST-PLAYED SONGS OF 2012

1. "Somebody that I Used to Know," by Gotye featuring Kimbra

2. "Call Me Maybe," by Carly Rae Jepsen

3. "We Are Young," by Fun.

4. "Payphone," by Maroon 5 featuring Wiz Khalifa

5. "Lights," by Ellie Goulding

Source: billboard.com

1.
PERSIAN

2.
EXOTIC

3.
MAINE COON

TOP 5

4.
RAGDOLL

5.
SPHYNX

MOST POPULAR
CAT BREEDS

Source: Cat Fanciers' Association

TOP 5
DREAM JOBS

What do you want to be when you get older? More than 8,000 people worldwide answered a survey about their childhood career aspirations. Here are the top responses. Did your dream job make the list?

1. Engineer 621 responses

2. Airplane or helicopter pilot 565 responses

3. Doctor/nurse/EMT 541 responses

4. Scientist 500 responses

5. Teacher 468 responses

Source: LinkedIn

TOP 5

Planets with the Longest Day

A day on Earth is 24 hours long. That's the average time it takes for the sun to move from its noon position in the sky back to that same position.

Source: NASA's National Space Science Data Center

1. MERCURY
175 Earth days, 21.6 hours

2. VENUS
116 Earth days, 18 hours

3. MARS
24.7 Earth hours

4. EARTH
24 hours

5. URANUS
17.2 Earth hours

TOP 5 Medal-Winning Countries

The 2012 Summer Olympics brought more than 10,000 top athletes to compete in London, England. Athletes from more than 204 countries competed. Below are the countries that won the most medals.

Source: london2012.com

1. United States
46 gold medals
29 silver medals
29 bronze medals
104 total

2. China
38 gold medals
27 silver medals
23 bronze medals
88 total

3. Russia
24 gold medals
26 silver medals
32 bronze medals
82 total

4. Britain
29 gold medals
17 silver medals
19 bronze medals
65 total

5. Germany
11 gold medals
19 silver medals
14 bronze medals
44 total

TOP 5 # Most Common Last Names in the United States

1. SMITH: 2,376,206 people

2. JOHNSON: 1,857,160 people

3. WILLIAMS: 1,534,042 people

4. BROWN: 1,380,145 people

5. JONES: 1,362,755 people

Source: U.S. Census Bureau

TOP 5 MOST GENEROUS COUNTRIES

A poll of more than 155,000 people in 146 countries studied charitable behavior. Based on that study, here are the world's most generous nations.

1. Australia

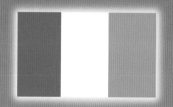

2. Ireland

3. Canada

4. New Zealand

5. United States

Source: Charities Aid Foundation, 2012 World Giving Index

TOP 5 GREATEST INNOVATORS

An innovator is a person who does something in a new way. More than 1,000 young adults were asked, "Who is the greatest innovator of all time?" Here's how they answered.

 TIE

5. Amelia Earhart 3%

Mark Zuckerberg 3%

4. Marie Curie 5%

3. Alexander Graham Bell 10%

1. Thomas Edison 52%

2. Steve Jobs 24%

Source: 2012 Lemelson-MIT Invention Index

TOP 5

PLACES TO BE A KID

A report from Save the Children ranked countries based on health, education, and nutrition. The lower the index, the more kid-friendly the nation.

1. JAPAN
.35 index

2. SPAIN
.55 index

3. GERMANY
.64 index

4. ITALY
.70 index

5. FRANCE
.74 index

Source: savethechildren.org

HOME-RUN HITTERS OF ALL TIME

1. **Barry Bonds** 762 home runs

2. **Hank Aaron** 755 home runs

3. **Babe Ruth** 714 home runs

4. **Willie Mays** 660 home runs

5. **Alex Rodriguez** 647 home runs

Source: mlb.com

TOP 5 LANGUAGES SPOKEN AROUND THE WORLD

1. MANDARIN
848 million speakers

2. SPANISH
406 million speakers

3. ENGLISH
335 million speakers

4. HINDI
260 million speakers

5. ARABIC
223 million speakers

Source: Ethnologue

1.
RUSSIA
6.60 million square miles
(17 million square km)

2.
CANADA
3.86 million square miles
(10 million square km)

Largest Countries

These countries cover the most territory.

3.
UNITED STATES
3.72 million square miles
(9.8 million square km)

4.
CHINA
3.71 million square miles
(9.6 million square km)

5.
BRAZIL
3.29 million square miles
(8.5 million square km)

Source: The CIA World Factbook

Gymnasts with the Most Olympic Medals

WOMEN

1. **Larisa Latynina** (Soviet Union*)
   18 medals

2. **Vera Caslavska** (Czechoslovakia**)
   11 medals

3. **Agnes Keleti** (Hungary)
   TIE **Polina Astakhova** (Soviet Union*)
   10 medals

4. **Nadia Comaneci** (Romania)
   TIE **Lyudmila Turischeva** (Soviet Union*)
   9 medals

5. **Sofiya Muratova** (Soviet Union*)
   TIE **Margit Korondi** (Hungary)
   8 medals

MEN

1. **Nikolay Andrianov** (Soviet Union*)
   15 medals

2. **Boris Shakhlin** (Soviet Union*)
   TIE **Takashi Ono** (Japan)
   13 medals

3. **Sawao Kato** (Japan)
   TIE **Alexei Nemov** (Russia)
   12 medals

4. **Viktor Ivanovich Chukarin** (Soviet Union*)
   11 medals

5. **Akinori Nakayama** (Japan)
   TIE **Vitaly Scherbo** (Belarus)
   Aleksandr Dityatin (Soviet Union*)
   10 medals

*In 1991, the Soviet Union was broken up into 15 countries, including Russia and Belarus.
**In 1993, Czechoslovakia was broken up into the Czech Republic and Slovakia.

Source: International Olympic Committee

TOP 5 LARGEST ISLANDS

1. Greenland
839,999 square miles (2,175,579 sq km)

2. New Guinea
341,631 square miles (884,824 sq km)

3. Borneo
290,320 square miles (751,929 sq km)

4. Madagascar
226,657 square miles (587,042 sq km)

5. Baffin Island
183,810 square miles (476,068 sq km)

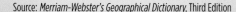

Source: *Merriam-Webster's Geographical Dictionary*, Third Edition

PHOTO CREDITS

Shutterstock.com (Kanchenjunga); Arsgera/Shutterstock.com (Lhotse); Vadim Petrakov/Shutterstock.com (Makalu). 48: Oleksiy Mark/Shutterstock.com (cargo train); Anatoly Tiplyashin/Shutterstock.com (Canadian flag, Mexican flag); Globe Turner/Shutterstock.com (Chinese flag, Japanese flag, German flag). 49: Monkey Business Images/Shutterstock.com (teens watching a movie). 50–51: NASA (all). 52: Library of Congress, Prints and Photographs Division (Theodore Roosevelt, Ulysses S. Grant); LBJ Library Photo by Frank Muto (John F. Kennedy); spirit of america/Shutterstock.com (Bill Clinton); Official White House Photo by Pete Souza (Barack Obama). 53: Library of Congress, Prints and Photographs Division (Ronald Reagan, William Henry Harrison, James Buchanan, Zachary Taylor); Department of Defense (George H.W. Bush). 54: Aaron Amat/Shutterstock.com (basketballs). 55: Sophie James/Shutterstock.com (Burj Khalifa); Jeffrey Liao/Shutterstock.com (Taipei 101); zhu difeng/Shutterstock.com (Shanghai World Financial Center). 56: Chatchada Thaprik/Shutterstock.com (planets). 57: Candis Davis/Shutterstock.com (beach). 58: Ben Heys/Shutterstock.com (huntsman spider); Giideon/Shutterstock.com (Brazilian salmon-pink spider). 59: Joel Sartore/National Geographic/Getty Images (Brazilian giant tawny spider); Audrey Snider-Bell/Shutterstock.com (goliath birdeater); linn/Shutterstock.com (wolf spider). 60–61: DanielW/Shutterstock.com (Library of Congress). 62: Sebastian Kaulitzki/Shutterstock.com (body). 63: pockygallery/Shutterstock.com (background); Steve Heap/Shutterstock.com (pie). 64: Markus Mainka/Shutterstock.com (background); Rafa Irusta/Shutterstock.com (chocolate pieces). 65: Tupungato/Shutterstock.com (background). 66–67: Anton_Ivanov/Shutterstock.com (Amazon). 68: Jacek Chabraszewski/Shutterstock.com (girl holding computer). 69: Weeraphon Suriwongsa/Shutterstock.com (cracked earth). 70: Stu Porter/Shutterstock.com (Thomson's gazelle); Peter Wey/Shutterstock.com (elk). 71: Stu Porter/Shutterstock.com (cheetah, wildebeest); ©Heather Patten/Dreamstime.com (pronghorn); Eric Isselee/Shutterstock.com (lion); Zuzule/Shutterstock.com (quarter horse). 72: Nagel Photography/Shutterstock.com (Yellowstone National Park); Jorg Hackemann/Shutterstock.com (Sequoia National Park). 73: Patrick Poendl/Shutterstock.com (General Grant/Kings Canyon National Park); Chiyacat/Shutterstock.com (Mount Rainier National Park); Anton Foltin/Shutterstock.com (Crater Lake National Park). 74: Indigo Fish/Shutterstock.com (boy). 75: pilgrim.artworks/Shutterstock.com (soda bottles). 76: Neftali/Shutterstock.com (Ronald Reagan); ra3rn/Shutterstock.com (Ulysses S. Grant); thatsmymop/Shutterstock.com (John F. Kennedy); Library of Congress, Prints and Photographs Division (Grover Cleveland); Stocksnapper/Shutterstock.com (Martin Van Buren). 77: Maks Narodenko/Shutterstock.com (mint leaves); alex saberi/Shutterstock.com (glasses). 78: ©FLPA/SuperStock (bar-tailed godwit); ©Glenn Bartley/All Canada Photos/SuperStock (common nighthawk); ©19838623doug/Dreamstime.com (blackpoll warbler). 79: nice_pictures/Shutterstock.com (Arctic tern); ©Glenn Bartley/All Canada Photos/SuperStock (sooty shearwater). 80: Artgraphixel.com/Shutterstock.com (Mexican flag); Globe Turner/Shutterstock.com (Puerto Rican flag, Cuban flag, El Salvador flag, Dominican Republic flag). 81: Comstock-Photos.com (boy with teacher). 82: Max Topchii/Shutterstock.com (girl on mountain). 83: National Oceanic and Atmospheric Administration/National Weather Service (Florida radar); Patsy Lynch/Federal Emergency Management Agency (Texas cars); Jocelyn Augustino/Federal Emergency Management Agency (Louisiana flood). 84: hecke61/Shutterstock.com (Brazil); ©John Warburton Lee/SuperStock (Democratic Republic of the Congo). 85: beltsazar/Shutterstock.com (Indonesia); Mariusz S. Jurgielewicz/Shutterstock.com (Peru); Rafal Cichawa/Shutterstock.com (Colombia). 86: WilleeCole/Shutterstock.com (bulldog); Lisa F. Young/Shutterstock.com (black dog); Suti gallery/Shutterstock.com (Pomeranian); Andresr/Shutterstock.com (golden retriever); Scorpp/Shutterstock.com (dog wearing sunglasses); Eric Isselee/Shutterstock.com (Labrador retriever, terrier); Erik Lam/Shutterstock.com (group of dogs); deamles/Shutterstock.com (all cats). 87: Anna Chelnokova/Shutterstock.com (boy with dog); Jaren Jai Wicklund/Shutterstock.com (fish); Marina Jay/Shutterstock.com (all birds); Subbotina Anna/Shutterstock.com (small animals). 88: Pressmaster/Shutterstock.com. 89: Solphoto/Shutterstock.com. 90: Luka Skywalker/Shutterstock.com (map).